Wile E. Coyote
Experiments with
ENERGY

by Suzanne Slade

illustrated by
Andrés Martínez Ricci

P9-CPW-247

CAPSTONE PRESS
a capstone imprint

Published in 2014 by Capstone Press
A Capstone Imprint
1710 Roe Crest Drive
North Mankato, Minnesota 56003
www.capstonepub.com

Library of Congress Cataloging-in-Publication Data
Slade, Suzanne, author.
Zap! : Wile E. Coyote experiments with energy / by Suzanne Slade;
illustrated by Andrés Martínez Ricci.
pages cm.—(Warner Brothers. Wile E. Coyote, physical science genius.)
Summary: "Uses popular cartoon character Wile E. Coyote to demonstrate science concepts
involved with energy"—Provided by publisher.
Includes bibliographical references and index.
ISBN 978-1-4765-4223-2 (library binding)
ISBN 978-1-4765-5214-9 (paperback)
1. Force and energy—Juvenile literature. 2. Force and energy—Experiments—Juvenile literature.
3. Science projects—Juvenile literature. 4. Wile E. Coyote (Fictitious character)—Juvenile
literature. I. Warner Bros. II. Title. III. Title: Wile E. Coyote experiments with energy. IV. Title:
Experiments with energy.
QC73.4.S57 2014
531.6—dc23   2013037000

Editorial Credits
Aaron Sautter, editor; Lori Bye, designer; Laura Manthe, production specialist

Cover and Interior Artist: Andrés Martínez Ricci

Capstone Press thanks Joanne K. Olson, Associate Professor of Science Education at
Iowa State University for her help in creating this book.

Table of Contents

Introduction:
Powered Up with Energy

Wile E. Coyote always has one thing on his mind—capturing that speedy, delicious Road Runner! Wile E. keeps trying out new inventions that use energy. But if he's ever going to succeed, he needs to understand how energy works.

Road Runner
(Speedius birdius)

Coyote
(Hungrius carnivorii)

Energy is the ability for something to do work, such as moving or lifting things. There are many kinds of energy, including electrical, chemical, mechanical, heat, light, and more. Wile E. knows that he needs a lot of energy to catch Road Runner. He just needs to learn which kind will work best and how to use it correctly!

Changing Energy

If Wile E. did his homework, he'd see that energy is all around him. He'd also see that energy often changes from one type into another.

Wile E.'s newest plan uses energy stored in **fuel** to help him soar after Road Runner. The engines in his ACME Flyer burn fuel. As it burns, the fuel's energy is changed into different types that can be used to do work. Some of the energy is turned into sound and heat. But the rest becomes mechanical energy that turns the Flyer's propellers and helps Wile E. fly through the air.

Wile E. thinks he's pretty smart. But he's forgotten something important. Fuel produces only a limited amount of energy. Once it's used up, it has to be replaced. Just as Wile E.'s stomach can't run on empty, his engines can't run without fuel. Too bad he forgot to bring some extra gas before he jumped off the cliff!

fuel—anything that can be burned to give off energy

Chapter 1: Energy in Motion

Spring into Potential

He doesn't realize it yet, but Wile E.'s next plan could cause him some trouble. He thinks his new ACME Super Spring will give him the boost he needs to grab Road Runner. His plan could work. But he needs to know more about how his spring works.

When Wile E. squeezes or stretches the spring, it gains and stores up **potential energy**. The more the spring is squeezed or stretched, the more potential energy it has.

potential energy—the stored energy of an object that is raised, stretched, or squeezed

Wile E. plans to use the spring's stored up energy to launch himself toward Road Runner. He wants to get moving fast, so he squeezes the spring as tight as possible. As Wile E. waits for Road Runner, the energy stored in the spring waits too. When he releases the spring, its stored energy changes into mechanical energy. The spring shoots out and quickly pushes Wile E. after Road Runner.

WHACK!

Unfortunately, Wile E. overlooked the second part of how springs work. As the spring pushes him forward, it stretches out and gains potential energy again. When the spring can't stretch any more, that energy again turns into mechanical energy. The spring quickly returns to its normal size and pulls Wile E. into the rock. Ouch!

On the Move

What's Wile E. up to now? He's fixing up a seedy snack with an extra surprise. Road Runner is always on the move, so Wile E. plans to get moving too. With his ACME Super Magnet and some iron birdseed, he's on the go in no time.

Kinetic energy is the energy of motion. Any type of motion—up, down, sideways, backward, or forward—is considered kinetic energy. The amount of kinetic energy an object has depends on its **mass** and speed. Mass is the amount of **matter** in an object. An object's kinetic energy increases if its mass or speed increases.

As Wile E. rolls faster and faster after Road Runner, his kinetic energy keeps increasing. Unfortunately for Wile E., other objects can have kinetic energy too. He's about to learn that a big train has tons of mass. This means that it has tons of its own kinetic energy too. Look out, Wile E.! That train isn't going to stop!

kinetic energy—the energy of things in motion
mass—the amount of material in an object
matter—anything that has weight and takes up space

Chapter 2: Electrical and Chemical Energy

It's Electric!

If Wile E. is going to catch the speedy Road Runner, he needs something with a lot more energy. He's sure that his new electric ACME Trap-O-Matic will bring success. Too bad there's nowhere to plug it in. Instead, Wile E. thinks he can hook his machine directly to the power lines running overhead. But that probably isn't the best idea.

To understand electricity, Wile E. needs to know about tiny particles called atoms. All matter is made up of atoms. Each atom has a **nucleus** made of protons and neutrons. Protons carry a positive electrical charge, while neutrons have no charge. Atoms also have negatively charged electrons that circle around the nucleus. Electrons can break free from atoms and flow between atoms in wires and other **conductors**. As the electrons flow, they create an electrical **current**. This electrical power can be used in many ways. When used properly, electricity is a safe and helpful source of energy.

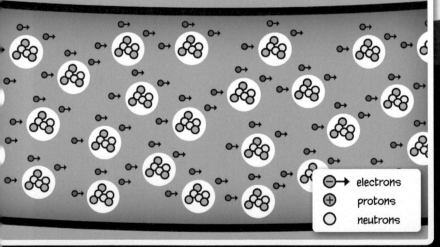

Electrical Current in Wire

⊖→	electrons	
⊕	protons	
○	neutrons	

nucleus—the center of an atom
conductor—a material that lets electricity travel easily through it
current—the flow of electrons

But Wile E. doesn't seem to realize how easily electricity flows through metal objects like wire. It can be very dangerous. Don't touch that wire, Wile E.! Oops, too late. Hopefully Wile E. learned a lesson. He should always keep his distance from electrical power lines.

ZAP!

Action! Reaction!

Wile E.'s first electrical scheme didn't work out. But this "Super Genius" thinks he knows how chemical and electrical energy work and is ready for action. When he fires up his battery-powered Super Scooter, the chase is on!

The battery in Wile E.'s scooter uses two different chemicals to create electrical energy. The chemical in the negative end of the battery carries extra electrons. The positive end has another chemical with too few electrons. The middle of the battery contains a barrier that keeps the two sides separate. When Wile E. connects his scooter's motor to the battery, electrons begin flowing to create an electrical current. The electrical power flows through the wires and the motor to make the scooter go.

Battery Power

Negative charge

Positive charge

electrical current   electrical current

Uh, oh! The battery in Wile E.'s scooter is dead. Too bad he didn't know that batteries don't last forever. Maybe next time he'll remember to use a fully-charged battery before chasing Road Runner.

OH NO!

Chapter 3: Heat Energy

Fuel the Fire

Wile E.'s battery-powered plan failed. But he's sure that his new plan using heat energy will work. He believes his powerful rocket will help him finally grab that tasty bird.

Wile E.'s rocket uses chemical fuel. When he lights the fuse, it starts a chemical reaction in the fuel's **molecules**. As the fuel burns, the bonds between the molecules break apart. The chemical energy stored in the fuel is changed to light, sound, and a lot of heat energy. The hot gases from the burning fuel are then forced out the back of the rocket. The process of burning the fuel changes its chemical energy into kinetic energy as the rocket blasts off.

Wile E. was right about one thing. The rocket fuel definitely provides a lot of energy. But it's a lot more than he was ready for. Wile E. should have remembered to use his seat belt!

WHOOSH!!

ANYONE HAVE A PARACHUTE?

molecule—two or more atoms bonded together to make the smallest unit of a substance

Hidden Heat

Wile E. has tried a lot of crazy ideas, but his plans never seem to work. Now he's thinking that a simpler plan might work better. This time he's going to use the heat under his feet to make some Road Runner soup. He just needs Road Runner to fall for his clever hot tub trick.

Deep inside Earth, temperatures reach up to 180,000 degrees Fahrenheit (100,000 degrees Celsius). These high temperatures create hot spots inside Earth's crust. These spots often create pockets of hot water and steam. Scientists drill into these pockets to capture Earth's natural **geothermal** energy. The hot water and steam is then used to spin **turbine generators** to create electricity. Geothermal energy can also be used to heat buildings. Some people even use natural hot springs for bathing.

Wile E.'s found the perfect place to cook up his dinner. It's just the right temperature for making delicious Road Runner soup. But he forgot one important thing—super-heated ground water also creates **geysers!**

CHOOOM!

Relaxing Hot Tub FREE for Road Runners

geothermal—relating to the intense heat inside Earth
turbine generator—a machine that produces electricity as a fluid passes through curved blades attached to it
geyser—an underground spring that shoots hot water or steam through a hole in the ground

Chapter 4: Renewable Energy Sources

Fun in the Sun

It's another hot day in the desert, and Wile E. is cooking up a new idea to get a mouthwatering dinner. He's hoping the sun will give his solar-powered car plenty of energy to catch up to Road Runner.

The fuel used in rockets or engines is nonrenewable. It can only be used once. But **renewable energy** sources like solar power are always available. Wile E.'s car is covered with solar panels. Each panel contains dozens of solar cells. When sunlight shines on the cells, a small amount of electricity flows between the layers inside. Thin metal strips in the cells capture this electricity and conduct it to larger wires. The electricity then flows to the car's motor. The motor then turns it into mechanical energy to power the car.

MEEP MEEP

Wile E. is off! He knows the sun won't run out of energy quickly like batteries or rocket fuel. But it looks like Wile E. is in the dark about how solar energy works. He needs to stay in the sunlight to keep his engine running!

renewable energy—power from sources that will not be used up, such as wind, water, and the Sun

The Wild, Wild Wind

Wile E. is ready to set sail in his latest contraption—the ACME Land Sailer. When the wind's energy pushes his sailer at high speed, Wile E. is sure that he can catch Road Runner this time.

As the sun beats down, it heats up the air above the desert. When the warm air rises, cooler air moves in to take its place. This air movement creates wind, which has a lot of energy that can be captured and used. Power companies use huge wind turbine generators to capture the wind's energy. The wind spins the turbine blades that are attached to the generator. The generator then changes the wind's energy into electrical energy to power homes and businesses.

SHWOOSH!!!

Wile E. knows that wind power is a renewable source of energy. But he must not realize that it isn't reliable or predictable. It can stop blowing, change direction, or be blocked. Without warning, the wind can start blowing again. Too bad for Wile E., the wind can also blow so hard it sends him sailing right over a cliff!

Wonderful Water Power

Ahoy, matey! Captain Coyote is riding the rapids to catch up with Road Runner. Wile E. knows the river has plenty of kinetic energy to get him moving. But he didn't know about that huge dam in front of him. Good thing he dove off his jet ski just in time!

But Wile E. isn't safe yet. He can't escape the water's strong current, which pulls him into the dam. This dam is part of a **hydroelectric** power plant. Water rushes through a long tube near the base called a penstock. The powerful flow of water pushes Wile E. around and around with the blades of a turbine generator. The generator turns the water's kinetic energy into electricity, which is sent to nearby homes. Like wind and solar power, hydroelectric power is another type of clean, renewable energy.

Luckily Wile E. is good at holding his breath! Don't worry Wile E. Maybe you'll have more luck catching Road Runner next time.

hydroelectric—having to do with making electricity from the force of moving water

Energy from Waste

In the desert, the nearest gas station can be hundreds of miles away. Wile E. learned earlier that energy in regular fuel can run out fast. But this time he's going to try using a biomass car instead. Biomass is a natural and renewable energy source made from animal and plant waste. Some cars run on bioethanol, which is a liquid fuel made from corn.

But Wile E.'s ACME Bio-Buggy 2000 is a super-fast experimental car. It can run on almost anything. As the car burns the biomass, the fuel's energy is turned into heat. That heat is then turned into mechanical energy to power the car. Fortunately for Wile E., there's plenty of biomass fuel available. He can use as much as he can find to power his new car.

Energy is Everywhere

Wile E. is one hungry coyote. So he keeps trying to use different kinds of energy to capture Road Runner. He has tried using mechanical energy, electrical energy, and chemical energy stored in fuel. He's tried renewable energy from the sun, wind, and water. He even tried using heat energy from deep inside Earth. But he still hasn't caught that pesky Road Runner. Could the ACME Solar Hover-Car finally be the answer?

Maybe not. Wile E. can't count on clear skies. However, he can always count on one thing—energy is found everywhere. Energy gives Wile E. the ability to do work and move things, and to keep chasing Road Runner.

WHY ME?

B LAM!!

Unfortunately, Wile E. still has a lot to learn about how energy works. It seems to be hazardous to his health!

Glossary

conductor (kuhn-DUHK-tuhr)—a material that lets electricity travel easily through it

current (KUHR-uhnt)—the flow of electrons

fuel (FYOOL)—anything that can be burned to give off energy

geothermal (jee-oh-THUR-muhl)—relating to the intense heat inside Earth

geyser (GYE-zur)—an underground spring that shoots hot water or steam through a hole in the ground

hydroelectric (hye-droh-i-LEK-trik)—having to do with making electricity from the force of moving water

kinetic energy (ki-NET-ik EN-ur-jee)—the energy of things in motion

mass (MASS)—the amount of material in an object

matter (MAT-ur)—anything that has weight and takes up space

molecule (MOL-uh-kyool)—two or more atoms bonded together to make the smallest unit of a substance

nucleus (NOO-klee-uhss)—the center of an atom

potential energy (puh-TEN-shuhl EN-ur-jee)—the stored energy of an object that is raised, stretched, or squeezed

renewable energy (ri-NOO-uh-buhl EN-ur-jee)—power from sources that will not be used up, such as wind, water, and the Sun

turbine generator (TUR-bine JEN-uh-ray-tur)—a machine that produces electricity as a fluid passes through curved blades attached to it

Read More

Biskup, Agnieszka. *The Powerful World of Energy with Max Axiom, Super Scientist.* Graphic Science. North Mankato, Minn.: Capstone Press, 2009.

Herweck, Don. *Energy.* Mission Science. North Mankato, Minn.: Compass Point Books, 2009.

Mullins, Matt. *Energy.* A True Book. New York: Scholastic, 2012.

Royston, Angela. *Energy for the Future.* Headline Issues. Chicago: Heinemann Library, 2009.

Internet Sites

FactHound offers a safe, fun way to find Internet sites related to this book. All of the sites on FactHound have been researched by our staff.

Here's all you do:

Visit *www.facthound.com*

Type in this code: 9781476542232

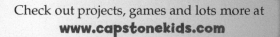

Super-cool stuff! Check out projects, games and lots more at **www.capstonekids.com**

Index